TRUE STORIES *of* ANGEL ENCOUNTERS

ANGELS
— All —
AROUND

By Lynn Valentine
with Bob Bubnis

Hallmark
gift books

PREMIUM
PRESS
AMERICA

TABLE OF CONTENTS

Introduction 1
The Man at the Back of the Room 3
From the Ashes.. 6
Following Orders 9
Amber's Angel.. 10
A Stone's Throw from Heaven 13
The Circle of Light.. 16
Dreaming Dreams and Seeing Visions........................ 18
The Reluctant Angel 20
Angel in the Eye of the Storm 23
Wake-up Call... 26
Angels Everywhere 28
Alright in the End 31
In the Blink of an Eye.. 33
Email Angel 34
Super Angel 37
Angel in the Water... 40
Angel by the Roadside.. 42
My Angel is Always Near....................................... 45
An Angel's Hands 47
From End to Beginning 51
Face to Face with an Angel 53
A Glimpse of Heaven 56
On a Mission from God 59
Finding Our Way.. 61

This is Only a Text.. 64
In the Twinkle of an Eye... 66
Angel on the Stairs 69
Protection from My Own Mistake 70
He is Listening, Always 72
Near Drowning... 74
Listen Well.. 76
A Lucky Brake.. 78
The Little Miracles.. 79
Walking Out of the Furnace 81
Raphael... 83

an-gel n. An immortal being attendant upon God;
        a very kind and lovable person;
        a helping or guiding spirit.

INTRODUCTION

Ten years ago I set out on a journey to find purpose, and in the process I found God; I found His angels; and I found myself.

Since then, that journey has taken me through some sad places and tough times, yet I still believe. I've had disappointments, frustrations, heartache and heartbreak, yet I still believe. Even over the course of writing this book, there were struggles, and yet still I believe.

Over these years, I've had the privilege of interviewing the people who passed along these incredible, amazing stories of divine interventions. In their words, it is apparent that God and His angels are at work in our lives. Sometimes they protect us from impending danger; sometimes they deliver a message from God; and other times they are there to comfort us.

I experienced that comfort recently when my mother passed away. She was courageous in her fight, and when it was clear that she was going to be with the Lord, she faced that fact with the bravery of a believer. As she lay dying, she took my hand in hers and assured me that she could go through what was ahead because she knew she would be with God in the end.

In the time I had left with her, I began to feel angry, lost and alone; and when Mom saw my heartache, she told me to be strong and know that God and His angels would take over and care for me because I still believe.

She was right.

I still believe!

It is on that note of belief that I'd like to introduce this book. I hope these stories of real people and angel experiences will inspire you and fill your heart with faith and hope. I'll begin with the tale of my own angel encounter…

Blessings,
LYNN VALENTINE

Behold, I send an Angel before

you to keep you in the way and

to bring you into the place

which I have prepared.

— EXODUS 23:20 —

The Man at the Back of the Room

⌁⌖⌁

I've been collecting stories and writing about miraculous encounters for many years now. As an author, I get the chance to speak at book signings and such; but I really don't like doing it. Don't get me wrong. I love talking to people who have stories of their own to tell, and I like spending time with those I have met along the way. My problem is that I don't really like to be the center of attention, especially when that attention rightfully belongs elsewhere. What's funny is that even though I am apprehensive about it, I always end up having fun whenever I go and drive away feeling blessed by the people I get to meet.

A few years ago, my publisher scheduled some book signings to coincide with my new book release. While I was a little reluctant to go, I was delighted to see that they were spaced out far enough to allow my friend Bob and me to have some fun along the way. We drove to St. Louis, Chicago, Nashville, Chattanooga, and Atlanta, stopping at the different landmarks along the way and making a real adventure out of it.

At our last signing, the middle of the store had been cleared out and a number of chairs were set up. There was a podium for me to lean on, making me feel more self-conscious about this than usual.

I always get nervous about these kinds of things. There is a chance that a skeptic is going to show up wanting to play devil's advocate and give me a hard time. There are those impossible questions to answer, like, "Why me?" I'm not a theologian, or a pastor; but even if I was, I don't think that's a question that any human being can really answer truthfully.

One other question I get is if I've ever had an angel encounter of my own. While I have, I have never actually seen an angel that I was aware of.

All I know and all I can come back to is that there is a future beyond this life that is worth looking forward to. Each person I interview, and every story I look into point to the fact that we are not alone, and that God wants us to know that His involvement in our lives is ongoing and didn't end with the Bible.

On the day of this particular book signing, I was relieved to see that only a small crowd had come to see me. Whether it was a bad night of the week, or the weather kept people at home, or poor promotion, I'm not sure. Just enough people showed up to keep it from being embarrassing, but not so many that I couldn't spend some time getting to know everyone.

I like to start a signing by reading a story out of one of the books and then I'll take questions, or speak for awhile about some of the people I've had the pleasure of meeting. Things went well, and I had a great time talking to everyone while signing some books, shaking hands and sharing some hugs.

Finally, when it was over, my friend Bob helped me collect my things while I thanked the manager of the store. On the way out though, Bob stopped me.

"Let me check things out first," he said.

Now Bob is protective and while I wouldn't call him paranoid to his face, he was acting like my personal bodyguard on high alert. When he was confident that we were safe, he walked me out to the car, all the time keeping a watchful eye on the parking lot.

As he got in the driver's side and shut the door, I could see him relax.

"So what did you think about Seth Plate showing up?" he asked.

I had no idea what he was talking about.

"You know, that tall guy in the back. He came in right after you read that story."

I was still at a loss. As I said, this was a small crowd, and I'm a pretty observant person; but I had no recollection of anyone coming into the gathering.

"Oh, come on, you couldn't miss the guy. He was tall, good-looking, dark-haired, wearing a trench coat. It was clear that he was trying to look like one of the angels from that movie, *City of Angels*."

I searched my mind but couldn't remember anyone who matched that description. *City of Angels* is one of my favorite movies, and I wouldn't have missed someone dressed like that.

Bob went on to say that the guy made him nervous. "His expression was serious," Bob explained. "And the whole time he didn't take a seat either, even though there were plenty of chairs. I couldn't help but worry. He just stood there, perfectly still, just waiting. Then, at the end when it was over, instead of getting a book signed, or going forward to meet you, he just left."

This did seem odd. Why would a person come out to see me and not meet me or get a book signed? My autograph isn't going to go get auctioned off at Christie's any time soon, but still, to come out to a signing and not get a signature seemed strange.

As I began to mull it over, I wondered if I didn't have my visitation. While I wished I would have seen him, maybe the thing I am supposed to get out of this is that it's okay if we don't see our guardian angels, as long as we don't forget that they are there.

—LYNN VALENTINE

From the Ashes

⟨⟩

Normally, nightmares are something that we wake up from. But during the early morning hours of Friday, August 1st, 1975, I woke up to one of the worst nightmares that a mother can face. My house was on fire.

I lived in a large five-bedroom home with my two daughters and five sons. My room was on the main floor near the room that my daughters shared, and my boys slept in the rooms upstairs. With no other adults in the house, I knew it would be up to me to get us out of this alive, so I rushed out of my room into the smoke and began screaming for everyone to get out.

The way the fire was spreading, I knew that I needed to get upstairs as quickly as I could. Shouting all of the way, I ran up the steps and burst through the doors where my boys were sleeping. I told them that the house was on fire, and that they could make it to safety if they would just hurry. As they got to their feet, I spun around and ran full speed to where my girls were.

The fire had grown in strength as it consumed our belongings, filling the place with hot, grey smoke. As I got to the girls' room, I saw three of my boys running by me, leaving two of their brothers behind upstairs. I focused on my daughters for the moment, getting one out the door and another on her feet. Just then I was thankful to see two more figures masked by the smoke, running past the door toward safety. With a strength I didn't know that I had, I got my daughter out after them.

Coughing, and with eyes stinging, I made it out of the inferno and onto the lawn. As soon as my vision cleared, I did a quick head count only to find six children. I looked around, frantically recounting, but one of my boys was still missing. Knowing I'd have to go back in, I turned toward the house just in time to see it explode.

By then the neighbors had come outside to see what was happening. I wanted to go back inside, but they restrained me. All I could do was watch helplessly as the flames grew under a twisting pillar of smoke.

I looked around again, hoping that I'd just missed him somehow, but he was nowhere to be found. My other kids were safe, however, sitting on the curb across the street with a stranger. He was talking calmly, and his manner seemed to keep them from being too upset as they watched the house burn.

The fire department showed up next and began to battle the blaze. The flames were so intense by now that I had given up hope that they could rescue my son. Still they fought bravely to contain it and keep it from spreading.

One of the firefighters noticed that the fire was inching toward my car. To keep the fuel from igniting, and to save at least one thing from the inferno, they went to move it out of the way. As they got in the car, I saw my seventh child pop up from the back seat. He had made it outside after all and had hidden inside the car for safety. I ran toward him, pulled him into a hug and sobbed with relief. While I was so grateful for the safety of my children, the shock of having my world go up in smoke was beginning to settle in. Not wanting to upset my boy any more than necessary, I let him rejoin his brothers and sisters and found a curb where I could sit down and cry it all out.

When I recovered enough to be myself again, I went to be with my kids. I needed to hold them, and I wanted thank the man who was sitting with them during this terrible ordeal; but by the time I got there, the man had gone. I didn't recognize him. As far as I knew, he didn't live in the neighborhood, so it was a mystery to me what he was doing there at that odd hour on a Friday morning. I asked if anyone knew who he was or where he had gone, but no one there had any idea. In the end,

I dismissed the whole thing as a chance encounter with a kind-hearted good Samaritan.

A few days later, I went back to the charred remains of our home and sifted through the ashes to see if there was anything left to salvage. It was an eye-opening experience to see how all of the things that we work so hard to get can be lost in a puff of smoke.

As I wandered through the blackened wood, melted plastic, and paper that had been turned into crumbling grey dust, I found one of my daughter's prized possessions, untouched by the flame and the heat. Then I found something of my son's, and then something else that belonged to another one of my kids. By the time I was done, I had recovered a treasured possession for each of us, including something for me. In the midst of all that I had lost, I found the box that I had kept some of my favorite things in, like cards, letters, and the first teeth of each of my babies.

Delighted, I rushed back to my kids with all that I had found. It was then that I learned something that amazed me so much that I wanted to share it with the world.

It seems that during the time my kids were on the curb with that mysterious man, he told them that he was sorry that they were losing so much. He then asked each of them what one thing they would miss the most.

Who he was remains a mystery, but I think that he might just have been an angel sent to watch over us, who figured as long as he was at it, he'd save a little something for each of us as a reminder of what is really important.

—Susan Stevens

Following Orders

When I was nine-years-old, something strange happened to me. Although it happened nearly five decades ago, the event is still as fresh in my mind today as it was back then.

My dad was in the Air Force and a part-time judo instructor. Despite being a very busy man, he would sometimes go out of his way to take me along with him when he needed to go somewhere. This included his judo class.

On one particular evening, I was playing with my toys, and was so into it that I didn't even notice when my dad started getting ready for class. He was heading for the door by the time I realized he was leaving. I didn't want him to go without me, so I started after him when I heard a voice say, "Don't ask him."

I was scared. The voice was loud enough to startle me, but what scared me most was that my mom and dad didn't hear it. It was powerful, and spoke with such authority that I chose to obey it, and let my dad leave without me.

Hours later, my dad returned in a taxicab. His hand and his nose were both broken, and he was bruised everywhere. It turned out that he had been in an accident with a semi-truck on the way to his judo class. The big rig wound up running up over the passenger side of my dad's pickup, completely crushing the place where I would have been that night. There was no way that anyone in that seat would have survived this wreck.

Later I told my mom about the voice, but she didn't seem to believe me. The important thing, though, is that I believed when it counted and did what I was told to do.

—Stephen Lynch

AMBER'S ANGEL?

⸻

Last year was horrible for me. Without going into all of the details, I was a distraught girl who'd lost my dignity, my self-esteem and my father—and I was only 17. Even worse than that though, somewhere along the way I lost my faith. I was still a Christian and I knew that God existed, but I wasn't sure He could say the same about me.

On October 2nd, 2006, I found out that I was wrong.

It was around 8:00 at night, when I decided to go out and buy a belated birthday card for a friend. I was eager to take my new car out for a ride, so this provided me with an excuse to get out for a while.

On the way home, my car began to act funny. In the beginning, it felt as if there was something being dragged underneath it, and then it began to lose power. I would press down on the gas pedal, pushing it all the way to the floor, but I couldn't get it to go more than 20 miles per hour.

I kept heading toward home, but soon it became apparent that the car wasn't going to make it. The engine began to cut out and eventually died as I entered a four-way stop. Thankfully I was able to coast it onto the shoulder of the road, just outside of the intersection before coming to a stop.

Safe on the side of the road, I got out of the car and inspected the vehicle as well as I could. The tires were all fine, and nothing seemed to be dragging on the road. Everything looked fine, so whatever was wrong with it wasn't something I could fix.

I didn't have a phone on me, but remembered seeing a pay phone outside of a laundromat about block away. I found some change, stashed my purse inside the car, locked it up and set out on foot.

It seemed especially dark as I began walking up the hill. As if this wasn't scary enough, I noticed a man in the shadows that seemed to be watching my every move. With every step that I took away from the car, I felt more vulnerable.

I began to hurry, and then decided to go across the street to get some distance between that man and me. That's when I crossed the street against the light and stepped into the path of an oncoming car.

I lost consciousness when I hit the street.

As it turned out, other than the concussion, I only had minor injuries and was released from the hospital that very night.

I called my Mom who rushed over to take me home. Once we were back at the house and able to relax, she asked me if I remembered anything about the accident. I told her that I didn't, but almost as soon as I said that, images began to form in my mind and suddenly I remembered everything.

I was lying in the road and couldn't move. It felt like I was trapped in my body. I wanted to get up leave, but I couldn't.

At my side appeared a woman who seemed to glow with a golden light. Looking down at me, she was speaking, or praying, but her words seemed muffled, like I was hearing them from under water.

She had this comforting way about her. She looked at me like she knew me, and in her eyes I felt total unconditional love.

I told the glowing woman that she was pretty, and she replied with words I could hear clearly that her name was Isabel, which means "God is my oath."

As we talked, the pain of what happened seemed to go away. Gone with it was the emotional pain that I had been suffering from before the accident. I felt myself healing.

I passed out, happy.

Why was I spared? I don't know. Maybe it was to tell this story and encourage others that there is something beyond this life. I may have lost my dad; but from my experience, I know that what we are goes on forever. God promised that, and God's oath is good enough for me.

—AMBER PEDERSONS

The Lord, before whom I walk,

will send His angel with you

and prosper your way.

– GENESIS 24:40 –

A Stone's Throw
from Heaven

⊷⊷

I was at one of those points in my life where no part of it seemed to be going right. I was unemployed, depressed, in debt, alone, and barely hanging on to the last thread, dangling at the end of my rope.

Not one to give up without a fight, I summoned up what strength I had and decided to do something about it. Realizing that getting back to work would fix a lot of what was wrong, I printed up some resumes, dressed up for possible interviews, and set out to change my life. I figured I'd mail most of the resumes. But there were a few companies that would be worth going to extra effort for, so I thought I would deliver resumes personally in those cases.

After a productive day of searching, I was beginning to feel a little better about myself. Just stepping out and trying was enough to give me hope that something good could happen. When I had gone to every place I could think of, I turned the car back onto the freeway that would get me home.

Cruising along the pass that was cut into a side of a mountain, I was replaying some of the events of the day. Suddenly my eyes locked in on a huge boulder that had come to rest in my lane. I veered out of the way, causing other cars to jerk away violently to avoid hitting me. All around me were the sounds of tires squealing. Despite my best efforts, I clipped the side of the rock and began to slide sideways. I fought to bring the car back under control, and by some miracle I was able to get all of the tires going the same direction again. The ordeal wasn't over yet though, as it quickly became apparent by the vibrations and the steady thump of limp rubber on the road, that somehow during the evasive maneuver my tire had gone flat.

Amazed that I wasn't dead, I coaxed my car to the shoulder. Between the boulder in front of me, and cars barreling down behind me, it felt like someone up there was aiming for me. Shaking, I remained behind the wheel, afraid to get out of the car. I closed my eyes and tried to calm my nerves. Before I could accomplish that, a rap on the window startled me. I looked outside to see a man standing there.

"Are you okay?" he asked.

"I'm fine, thank you."

"I saw the whole thing," he said. "What happened to you was not by chance. This was an act of God."

I failed to see what purpose God would have for throwing a boulder at me, but wasn't in any condition to argue about it.

The man then asked if I had a spare tire and offered to change it for me. Still shaking too much to do it myself, I decided to take him up on his offer. I got out of the car and opened the trunk, cautioning him to be careful as we were still on a busy freeway. He just smiled, and told me not to worry because God was protecting him.

As he jacked up the car, he was completely oblivious to the cars rushing past us. Over the sound of the traffic, he went on to say that God had a message for me. "God wants you to know that everything is going to be alright in your life. It is all going to work out. Just keep praying."

He went on to tell me about a young girl who was cured of a disease after she turned her life over to God. I politely listened; after all, I was a captive audience at this point.

Once the car was off of the jack, and everything was snuggly put away in the trunk, I went to get my purse from the car so that I could offer him something for his trouble. When I turned back to thank him though, he was gone. This completely shocked me, because there wasn't enough time for him to have gotten into a car to drive away.

I went home and cried. The stress of the near miss combined with all of the stress I was feeling anyway. I was even more emotional after hearing the words of a man that I didn't know, telling me that the God I had doubted, still cared. The emotions had nowhere else to go but in my tears. The Bible says in Psalm 56:8 that God catches all of our tears and saves them in a bottle. I let go of all of that pain and let God catch it. As I cried, the words of that man cleared it up for me. That a job might be the answer to a lot of my problems, God is the answer to all of them.

About half an hour later, I got in the car, and went back to that same spot on the freeway. To my surprise, the boulder was gone. I looked along the side of the road, but there was no trace of it anywhere.

Maybe sometimes God puts a boulder in our way on purpose to get our attention.

—MARTIKA

THE CIRCLE OF LIGHT

Surgery is one of the scariest things we ever have to face. Aside from the fear of having to deal with whatever is physically wrong with us, being on that operating table means completely surrendering to others and trusting your life in their hands. In regular everyday life, people have to earn our trust over time before we allow ourselves to be vulnerable to them. But in the operating room, time is measured in heartbeats. You have to give in. Once you realize that you have no other choice, all you can do is pray, or in the case of non-believers, "hope for the best."

Even as believers though, we don't always know how to pray. Sometimes we lack the words. Some people bargain while others beg, and others just groan, hoping that God will know what they mean.

In my case, when major surgery became my only option, I found myself completely unable to pray, beg, bargain, or groan. Even though I am a praying woman, I just couldn't find the words or the strength to go before the Lord and ask Him for His blessing.

Not wanting to face this without prayer, I turned to friends at church and got them praying for me, hoping that my prayers would join theirs before the big day came.

This prayer block continued for several days until finally I ran out time. With the operation just hours away, I decided to give it another try and ask the Lord for His help. Just as I was getting ready to close my eyes, I saw a light form in the room. Looking closer, I could see it was a circle of light with an angel standing in its center. As I looked at it, all of my fears began to dissipate. My anxiety was replaced by peace, and my worries were smoothed away by the absolute belief that God answers even the unspoken prayers of our hearts. I realized that I wasn't trusting a doctor, or being vulnerable to him, but rather trusting God instead. The angel disappeared, and when it was over, I was ready for whatever happened next. After all, the worst that could happen is that I would be with God.

In the end, I never did get the chance to pray. I didn't have to. God had a plan all along. He was just waiting for me to bow my head before He would let me in on what He was doing.

Needless to say, the surgery went well, and ever since then, I've been thankful for the fact that I am in God's circle of friends.

—SHARYN

DREAMING DREAMS AND
SEEING VISIONS

~~◆~~

Not being able to see the forest through the trees is a great description of how we often regard the blessings in our lives. Sometimes we are just not able to see miracles that are happening all around us because we are so focused on the problems that prayer is still working on. During those times, it's good to have friends and family in the faith help us see our lives in perspective—from the outside, where God's work is sometimes more evident.

I have a condition called hydrocephalia, which is an abnormal accumulation of cerebrospinal fluid in the ventricles, or cavities, of the brain. This is very dangerous as it can cause excessive pressure in the skull leading to all kinds of terrible things like convulsions, mental disability and even death. Because of this, I needed surgery to place a shunt system in my head that would allow this fluid to drain out. I was already in a critical situation and needed to get in right away. This was one of those times that I was not able to see that God was at work.

While I was being operated on in Tampa, Florida, however, my grandfather, who lived an ocean away in Durban, South Africa, had a vision. He felt so strongly about what he had seen that he wrote me a letter.

> *Dear Beverly,*
>
> *I am writing this to tell you what I saw when you underwent the surgery.*
>
> *I saw three Angels around you. One stood on either side of you, stroking your arms and talking to you, telling you not to be afraid and that the Lord will hear you. They were dressed in*

light peach colored clothes, and they seemed to be happy as they spoke to you.

The third Angel stood at the head of the bed, directing the surgeon, telling him exactly what to do. (Praise the Lord). A fourth Angel was comforting your Mom and Dad with its wings spread over them, telling them not to fear as "God is in Control."

I was in a coma for few weeks afterward and had to learn how to walk and talk again, but now I am able to thank Him for watching out for me, and giving my grandfather a brief glimpse behind the veil.

—BEVERLY KNIGHT

THE RELUCTANT ANGEL

I am a missionary. I have traveled through over forty countries, doing the Lord's work with my family wherever we are called to go. In that time, we've met some very nice people; and, along the way, we have crossed paths with at least one angel that I know of.

Our encounter happened when my wife and I were in Sao Paulo, Brazil. There was a Christian convention that we needed to attend. It was around sixty-miles away, so my wife and I did what we usually do when we don't have access to a car. We had faith that God would get us there. While Brazil has a really good transportation system, our favorite way to travel is hitchhiking. Not only is it a less expensive way to travel, but it also gives us the opportunity to strike up conversations with people along the way, allowing us to minister and share our faith with them.

The drawbacks of this mode of transportation, however, are that it might take awhile to get a ride, and summers get extremely hot in Brazil. We must have looked ridiculous, walking in the heat of the day as perfectly good buses drove by us with vacant seats on them. Still we pushed on, walking with our thumbs out, and waiting in faith that the driver God had planned for us was on his way.

As the sun climbed in the sky, the temperature reached the point where it was almost too much to endure. I prayed for relief, which the Lord provided with some welcome cloud cover. While I was grateful for the break from the sun, I was really hoping that God would send us a ride. We were tired, hot, and hungry by now, and wishing we could be with our friends at the conference.

About then, a dilapidated truck coming from the opposite way stopped. The driver motioned for us to get in.

I was a bit confused as he wasn't even going our direction, but I felt compelled to accept his offer. As we sat down in the squeaky old seats next to him, he introduced himself as Elias which is the same as Elijah in English.

We told him where we were going, but he told us gruffly that he already knew and acted as if we were stating the obvious. He turned the old heap around and started down the road toward our destination.

We couldn't really speak to him as we normally do in these situations, as the truck was backfiring and making so much noise. So we quietly bounced down the road, trying to enjoy the ride, happy to be on our way.

After awhile, as we got closer to the conference, I was beginning to get hungry and thought we should get off for a bite to eat. We were passing some restaurants that I knew I could afford, so I waited for him to get off of the accelerator and spoke up when the engine quieted a little. "We're hungry and would like to stop and get something to eat."

Again, he acted as if he already knew this but continued to pass restaurants we could have stopped at. It was as if I had said nothing.

Finally, he pulled over to a restaurant we didn't even know about and shut off the engine. He told us that we could get a good meal here, and that it would be free. Confused, we got out, thanked him, and he drove away. As he left, we noticed he had no plates on the truck. In Brazil, this is something the police are very strict about. The other thing they don't tolerate are cars that make excessive noise. This gave him two strikes. It seemed odd that we would make the trip completely unnoticed by the regular road patrols.

When we got in the restaurant, it was empty, but there were many tables set up as if they were preparing for a large banquet with hundreds of guests. The owner welcomed us in with a big smile and directed us to a table where he presented us with menus. We explained we were missionaries, but he remained completely at ease and continued to treat us as if we were royalty. At the end of the meal, when we were full and refreshed, he let us know that our meal was free, and we left thankful and happy.

The very next vehicle that came along stopped to give us a ride and got us to the conference.

When we arrived, we told our friends about our "know-it-all" friend who saw to our every need after our prayer. They were convinced, as we were, that the one who really does know it all sent a reluctant angel by to give us a lift and treat us to a meal fit for the children of the King.

—MICHAEL JAFFRAY

Angel in the Eye
of the Storm

Hurricane Isabel came to the Chesapeake Bay determined to remind everyone of just how powerful nature can be. It was the second major hurricane of the season and would prove to be the biggest one of the year. It was so large that its effects were felt from Long Island to the tip of the Florida peninsula.

Unlike a tornado that can just drop from nowhere, or an earthquake that just suddenly happens, it takes nature a little while to build up for a hurricane. As a veteran of many of these, we listened when the warnings came to get out of her way.

We packed our car with as much as we could fit inside of it, trying to focus on the things that really mattered the most. Then, with the clouds looming in the distance, we collected our three pets and made the trip inland to my son's house. He was far enough from the coast where we knew we'd be safe from the full brunt of Isabel's fury.

The hurricane grew to a category five storm, with winds in excess of 165 miles per hour. Although it had weakened some as it hit the land, it was still more than a match for many of the structures in her path. Buildings shook and splintered against the winds, giving way as the hurricane came down on our little community. When she was done raging, 16 people had lost their lives and 300 homes were destroyed, including ours, leaving lifetimes of memories and belongings floating in the water.

The day after Isabel was gone, we went back to clean up and salvage what we could. Knowing in advance from the news footage that our home was probably lost, we left our pets behind with my son and set out on the long terrible journey. We were grief stricken to see the piles of rubble where our community used to be.

While human life is by far more important than possessions, nothing can quite prepare you for losing everything. Pictures, video, and keepsakes passed down from distant generations were lost forever.

Still we were able to find some of our things and begin the long task of sorting out what we could save. As I stood knee deep in water, trying to find anything of value, I was at the edge of what I could handle emotionally.

Then as the sun went down, I got a phone call from my son that made the day even darker. My 10-year-old poodle KC was missing; and, despite all of their efforts to find her, she was nowhere to be found.

The thought of losing her was too much to bear, so I begged God to send His angels to guide my son and help him find KC before something happened to her.

Feeling responsible, he went out looking for her again. He called her name, going farther into the night, straining to hear the sound of her bark, while watching for the glimpse of her fur in the distance. By the time he gave up, he realized that he had wandered so far that he was lost, too. He had made it into another neighborhood that he wasn't familiar with and didn't have any idea of where he was.

As he looked around to try to get his bearings, he suddenly saw KC, sitting in someone's yard next to a statue of the Virgin Mary.

Our prayers had been answered.

When you think about it, this really was miraculous. My son could have wandered down any one of a hundred streets; and yet, he was directed to the one path that led him to the exact spot where KC was waiting. The fact that she was sitting next to the statue only puts an exclamation point on the miracle.

The moral of this story is that if we begin a journey in prayer, even when we feel lost, we are right where God wants us to be.

—LISA S.

But at night an angel of the Lord opened the prison doors and brought them out, and said, "Go, stand in the temple and speak to the people all the words of this life."

— ACTS 5:19-20 —

WAKE-UP CALL

Sometimes things happen in life that make it hard to be a believer. I was raised up in church and always wanted to be a good man. But when I was just 21 years old, I lost both of my parents, and I blamed God for it. It was in His power to stop it, and He didn't. Because of that, I was full of anger and resentment, feeling abandoned, alone, and unworthy of His love.

Things continued to spiral downward as I had one failed marriage behind me, with another one to follow; and then, to complete my misery, I found myself in jail, awaiting trial for a murder I didn't commit.

One day while I was sitting in jail, thinking back on the sad condition of my life, a man came up and asked me to join him and a few of his friends for a Bible study.

My first thought was to pass judgment on the man. He was in for murder, and now he was having a Bible study? It occurred to me then, however, that I was in for the same crime, and probably didn't have any room to talk. How quick we are to judge others. I reluctantly agreed to attend.

About halfway through the study, an elderly man came up to me and began to quote scriptures. His eyes seemed to look through me, past my tough façade and into my soul. His voice gave me chills as the conviction of his words blew past my defenses. What shocked me the most though was when he called me by my first name. I had not told anyone my first name. In jail you go by last names and numbers.

"William," he said. "You will be in jail for a while, but have faith and be patient because everything is going to work out."

There are times when you think something spiritual might have happened in your life, and then there are times that you know something spiritual happened. That night, when I went to bed, I knew something divine had happened. I prayed to God from my bunk, and apologized for turning away from Him. I asked for forgiveness, and knew that I had received it. When I closed my eyes and slept, it was the best sleep I had experienced in years.

The next morning, I went to look for my new friend, but he was nowhere to be found. I asked all of the inmates, but no one knew who I was talking about. I asked the deputies, and they said they didn't know of anyone answering that description. To say that everyone thought I was a nut is putting it mildly. No one even wanted to speak to me after that. But it was okay because of what the stranger had told me. It gave me more time to pray and to read my Bible.

I waited patiently for eight months for my trial to begin, having complete faith that everything would turn out for the best. The day before my trial, my accuser recanted her story. The case was dismissed, and I was free.

Thanks to my experience in jail, I now work toward the freedom of other people who are falsely accused. I tell everyone in and out of jail about my experience and hope they will learn a little something about judging, repenting, and believing. Who knows? The next person you judge might just be the angel that is coming to set you free.

—WILLIAM STRUTZ

Angels Everywhere

My husband Bob and I had been watching television together one night when I began to feel really tired. I tried to fight off the urge to sleep, but my eyelids proved too heavy to keep open. Exhausted, I headed downstairs to bed as Bob got up and performed his rounds, turning off lights and checking the doors.

Before I could turn the sheets, I noticed a dull ache in my left arm. It was a sensation I had never felt before, and it caused me to become quite concerned. I went back upstairs and told Bob that I didn't fell well.

He was done securing the house, so he followed me downstairs while I described the feeling. As we went into the bedroom, I heard an odd buzzing sound. The noise seemed to be coming from somewhere in the room, but I couldn't figure out from where.

I went to the bathroom, but the buzzing was still there and just as loud as it was before. When I asked Bob if he could hear it too, he grabbed his wallet and his keys and said, "I am getting the car. You need to go to the hospital."

Thankfully the hospital was only about two blocks away, so it didn't take long for Bob to get me there. As he got me inside, he told the man behind the desk that I was having a heart attack.

They mobilized quickly, taking me directly into the ER where the cardiac team started working on me. They went in and out of the room, connecting me to monitors and tubes and electrodes, doing what they are trained so well to do, until finally I had been stabilized.

When things calmed down, I closed my eyes and wondered if this was the end for me. Just then, as that thought entered my mind, a male voice answered me as if reading my mind.

"Everything is going to be alright," he said.

"How do you know?" I asked as I opened my eyes. To my amazement, I was completely alone in the room.

Not long after, they moved me to the Intensive Cardiac Care Unit. I was feeling better by then; and, with the monitors all watching over me, it seemed like a good idea to send my husband home. I couldn't sleep knowing he was sitting up in an uncomfortable chair somewhere in the hospital, waiting for news about me. When he was on his way, I let myself relax and finally found the sleep I was hoping for on the couch, hours before.

My rest ended at 6:30 a.m. when I woke up in distress. My face seemed to be hot. I began feeling some of what I felt before, with the numbness and buzzing sound. I pushed the button for the nurse. I was having a second attack and going into cardiac arrest.

The doctor said I needed a stent because the right artery was 100% blocked. There were only two hospitals available who could do the procedure. Time was running out, so we chose the closest one. I was moved by ambulance for a twenty-minute ride and had two stents put in.

The next morning, I was in a private room recovering when the nurse brought a copy of the book, *Angels Everywhere*, to me. She said that someone had left it at the nurses' station the night before with instructions to give it to me the next morning. The whole time I read it, I was wondering who would have left it for me.

A few days later I was released and went home where I received a call from one of the nurses. She inquired how I was feeling and if I was getting a lot of rest. She stated that she was curious if I had gotten to visit with my relative the morning of my cardiac arrest.

"What do you mean?" I asked. "What relative?" I had no family there at that time. My husband was home until the nurse called him and my daughter didn't even know that I was in the hospital until later.

The nurse proceeded to tell me that early in the morning, before I went into cardiac arrest, a tall, thin gentleman was standing outside my room. She said that she asked if she could help him, but he ignored her. She persisted and asked what business he had at the hospital. He looked at her and said, "I am family."

That was when the Code Blue was called. After that she didn't see him again. My husband was called; and he arrived a few minutes later, but the man who was by my door was gone. So the nurse was wondering if he ever did catch up with me.

Looking back on that day, it went without saying I was blessed. But it was clear to me that I was being watched over as well. There was the voice in my ear when I was alone. Then there was the man standing guard outside of my door.

My thinking was that he was an angel, who was there to remind me I am in the family of God; and then, just for fun, he left something to read as a calling card.

—Patsy Weikart

ALRIGHT IN THE END

It all happened on a summer day that was just too beautiful to waste. My friend Jackie and I decided to take advantage of it, and shopping seemed like the perfect way to enjoy ourselves. Without a care in the world, we took off down the freeway that would lead us to our first stop.

We weren't the only ones out looking for fun either. The lanes were filled with people off to lunch, movies, malls, and lakes. Just ahead of us, in fact, was a truck pulling a boat on a trailer, off to some adventure on a nearby waterway.

When we came up alongside the boat, however, something went wrong. The driver decided to change lanes, and it was clear by the way he was moving that he had forgotten that he had a boat in tow. As the trailer started to merge into our lane, I only had a few options. I could hit the brakes and get rear ended, or I could let him hit us and hope that he'd notice the jolt, or I could try for the shoulder and hope to come to a stop without hitting anything. In the split second I had to decide, I picked the shoulder.

As we left the road and started into the grassy median, all I could think of were Jackie's and my husbands and how bad they would feel when they found out what happened to us. I also wondered if we would feel pain.

At that moment, I felt the car lift up. Not fly up. *Lift up*. It felt like it was under control. We were still moving sideways, but we were not flipping—something seemed to be holding us steady. It was at that time that I heard someone say, "Don't worry, everything will be alright." The voice was clear, calm, strong and assuring.

When the car stopped, we were resting safely on all four wheels.

Amazingly, after my hands quit shaking, I found that the car drove just as well as it did before. I waited for the traffic to clear enough for me to safely ease back onto the freeway again and got off at the next exit to check out the car. There wasn't even a mark on it.

Why were we spared when we should have wrecked? I don't know. Maybe it was so that others could read this story and know that everything is going to be alright in the end.

—Sandra Hyler

For there stood by me this night an angel of the God to whom I belong and whom I serve.

– Acts 27:23 –

In the Blink of an Eye

～✖～

My son was very sick. His fever had hit 104°, and I was beginning to grow very afraid for him. I knew that anything over should get medical attention, so I watched him carefully, prayed, and comforted him as much as I could with cool rags on his forehead. I waited for the fever to break.

As I sat there with him, I got the idea to light his Baptism Candle. I left him just for a moment, went downstairs and lit the candle. I bowed my head and prayed that God would send healing to my son.

When I was done, I went to the kitchen for a glass of orange juice and started back up the stairs. As I got closer to the room, I began to feel something in the air. It was like the atmosphere was charged with electrical energy. The hairs on my arms and the back of my neck even began to stand on end. Not knowing what it was, I hurried to my son's room and opened the door to see a glowing being hovering over his bed. It seemed to be made completely of light and reminded me of an angel. Although I didn't make a sound, it seemed to notice me. In the blink of an eye, it was gone.

The next morning, my son was fine. He didn't have any recollection of what had happened the night before, but I have never forgotten.

Since then, I have come to see that as a visitation of a guardian angel sent in reply to a prayer.

—Arline Cahill

EMAIL ANGEL

———— ❧ ————

We have it within us to withstand a great many things, but sometimes we forget that. We start selling ourselves short, not realizing that our faith can outlast our strength. Joy will outlast sorrow, and ultimately everlasting life will outlast death.

The problem is that we don't see time the same way as God does. We see our limits at one place, but sometimes growth is a little further beyond that point. Sometimes the lesson is to have faith that God will fix things when something doesn't go our way.

I'm a man who has always believed in God, and I know that His power is great enough to overcome any obstacle. I had reached a point in my life, though, where I really needed Him to come through for me. But no matter how much I prayed, I heard no answer.

I lost my job because of corporate cut-backs. As a result, I lost my car, my house, and my insurance. My wife became ill, and I couldn't pay for her to get the tests and treatment that I knew she needed. She kept telling me that she was fine, but I knew better. Then the unthinkable happened. She had a stroke and lay helpless in a coma for days until a clot burst and she died. I never even got to say goodbye.

I was completely overtaken with grief. I knew that taking my life was wrong, so one Sunday night I went to church with one last prayer. The sanctuary was empty, so I went to the front, knelt down at the altar, and begged God to just take my life. It was worthless to me.

As I sat broken and crying, with my eyes closed, I felt someone come near me. You know that feeling when you can't see anyone but the air changes somehow? That was the feeling I had. I knew someone was there.

I figured it was just a member of the church who had seen me, or maybe my Pastor coming along to pray with me. Before I could look up, a soft male voice spoke to me saying, "Keep your eyes closed. Keep in prayer to your God. He hears you and He cares." Just then I felt a wave of perfect peace comforting me. It covered me like a blanket. For the first time in so long, I felt relief from the pain.

I looked up to see that no one was there. I turned around to see a woman sitting a few rows behind me, but she looked at me suspiciously as I stood to see if anyone else was nearby.

I asked her where the man had gone who had just spoken to me.

"Who are you talking about?" she asked, more confused than suspicious at this point. "I haven't seen anyone near you. We're the only ones here."

When I told her what had happened, she looked at me and smiled the biggest smile. Then she began to laugh one of those partly cloudy laughs, the kind that is mixed with crying and tears. She seemed to be dealing with her own pain as the joy seemed to overcome her sorrow.

I asked her if she was okay, and she came over next to me.

"Do you believe in angels?" she asked enthusiastically.

"Yes," I replied, wondering what she was getting at.

"The voice you heard had to have been that of your guardian angel. God uses angels to bring messages to us directly from heaven when a solution is needed immediately."

As I processed what she was saying, she compared an angel's message with that of an email versus a letter through the postal service. "An angel gets the message delivered faster."

We both laughed. After all I had been through, I was laughing again.

She had come to pray about her life, too, but what happened to me made her feel better as well. We both began to feel good about our futures, about God's purpose, and the fact that He cares about us. I have a purpose on this earth after all. I don't know what it is yet, but after getting that email, I guess I'll have plenty of time to find it.

—LESTER COLT

SUPER ANGEL

―――⊗―――

My best friend is one of the most dependable people you could ever meet. He does exactly what he says he is going to do, every time without fail. This trait is even more noticeable at work where he inadvertently makes everyone else look bad. He's never late, never leaves early, and even when he is not feeling well, his boss can count on seeing him ready for work.

Not surprisingly, one day he came into the office, even though he was feeling very sick. Concerned for his boss, and not wanting to let her down, he showed up at work, on time as usual. When his boss saw him though, it was clear that he should be resting. So she insisted that they would get along fine without him, and that he should go home. He reluctantly agreed but before he left, he promised her that he would be back to work the next morning.

When he got home, he laid down on the sofa, hoping to sleep it off. In a short time, however, he started to feel even worse. Before he could call for help, he lost consciousness.

The next day, when my friend didn't show up for work, his boss got concerned. She tried calling, but there was no answer. After several attempts to reach him, she became worried and pulled his file to find his address. Rather than call the police and risk scaring him if he were only sleeping, she decided to drive over herself and speak to the landlord or apartment manager about checking on him.

As she came up the steps, she found a man with a huge set of keys in a maintenance man's uniform standing at the top of the stairs. She asked if he was the building's superintendent, and the man said that he was. Relieved, she asked if he could check on her friend, explaining that he never missed work, especially without calling. Although she wished she could stay to find out if he was okay, time was getting away from her and she had to get back to the office. She didn't leave though until she got the man to promise to look in on him soon.

The super found my friend on the sofa—pale, cold, sweating and unconscious. A 911 call was made; and when the ambulance driver arrived, the super was there at the top of the stairs, leading the way to the apartment. They said later that my friend was in such bad shape when they got to him that the coroner would have had to be called if it would have gone on any longer.

When the paramedics turned back around to take some information from the super, there was no one standing there.

Several days later when my friend was released from the hospital, he thanked his boss for caring enough about him to take action. Then he went to the manager's office to thank the landlord and the super for checking up on him and calling 911.

The landlord didn't know what my friend was talking about. He said that he was over in another building across town, taking care of some maintenance problems on that day. He had no idea who could have gotten in with the key because he had the only key ring with him the whole time.

I told my friend there was only one explanation, and that was that his guardian angel was the one to make the 911 call and to open the door and lead the paramedics to the right apartment.

—JONATHAN SHRECKER

A Man of God came to me, and
His countenance was like the
countenance of the Angel
of God, very awesome; but I
did not ask Him where He was
from, and He did not tell me
His name.

– JUDGES 13:6 –

Angel in the Water

———◦•◦———

Just before I turned 16 years old, I went to California to spend the summer with my Grandmother. I had grown up in California and had been homesick for it ever since my parents moved us to Washington State.

Knowing that the summer would be over all too soon, I decided to make the most of every day that I had there. I immediately reconnected with old friends and, in no time, had a trip to the beach lined up with my friend Gina and some boys she knew.

I wanted to get to the ocean and feel the water on my skin again. I missed the smell of it, the sound of it, and the peaceful way it made me feel when I was near it.

By the time we got to our destination, the setting sun was skipping across the waves, creating a road of glittering diamonds aimed directly at me. I got Gina to go with me for a swim right away while there was still light enough to enjoy it.

We ran in the sand. It was loose and slowed us down as it gave way underfoot. It got harder and colder as we got nearer to the water, allowing us pick up speed until we could hop into the cold water. Even though I knew that it would be chilly, my skin was surprised and delighted by the coldness of it. I laughed and squealed as Gina and I splashed like kids in the waves. I plunged in and swam, enjoying the sense of freedom that it gave me.

Along with the coolness of the water, another thing that I had forgotten was just how powerful the undertow could be at night. The peaceful allure of the ocean had given way to its fierce power, and before I knew it, I was out too far, calling out to Gina to help me.

As I continued to drift away, Gina made her way to the shore to get help, but it seemed like it was taking forever for her to get there. I fought to stay afloat and tried to swim toward her, but my best effort didn't get me any closer to safety.

I was so afraid. Who are we to think we can play with a force as powerful and deadly as an ocean? I fought for a while, but soon became tired. It seemed that each wave that came over me left me under the water a little longer.

I began to relax and looked up through the water to see the glowing moon. I remember talking to God, but I wasn't asking Him to save me. I just wanted to tell Him how much I loved my parents and my Grandmother. I remember wishing that I could have been a better daughter.

Just then, I felt a powerful tug at my left arm with a force so strong that I thought my arm had been pulled out of its socket. The next thing I remembered, I was throwing up water while lying on a beach surrounded by people whose faces I could not make out. When my head cleared, I asked what had happened. Someone told me that a man named Michael saved my life and pointed at a figure walking away on the beach. He was tanned and blond and built like a surfer. Before I could get up and thank him, he disappeared before my eyes. He just vanished.

—ANONYMOUS

ANGEL BY THE ROADSIDE

I was on my way to a date with a young lady I had recently met. It was a first date, so I really wanted it to be special. I cleaned my new Camaro, dressed up nice, and headed out to my sister's house to pick up some flowers for her.

My sister had recently moved, and I had only been there one time before during the day. As it got dark though, I wound up making a wrong turn somewhere and found myself on a narrow asphalt road in the middle of nowhere.

It was sort of a creepy place with a dark forest on one side and an old junkyard on the other. It was protected by a barbed wire fence. For as far ahead as I could see, there wasn't an intersection or a place to turn around. It was the perfect set for a horror movie.

It was getting late enough that I started to worry about not getting to my date on time. Not knowing how far ahead I'd have to go before I found a place to turn around, I decided to do a three point turn in the middle of the road, gradually going back and forth on the narrow strip, just inches at a time, to get the car pointed in the opposite direction.

This would have been a tricky maneuver even in the daytime on dry streets, and it was doubly difficult at night after the rain. Still, I carefully kept working it back and forth, gradually making the turn. The road was narrower than I initially perceived it, however; and at one point, the front tires slipped off of the edge of the road, and I felt the car bottom out with a sickening "thud."

I made several attempts to get the car back on the road, but nothing worked. Out there in the middle of nowhere, I didn't have much hope of anyone passing through, let alone a tow truck or someone who could help me. On top of that, it was 1984, which was long before the introduction of cell phones.

I was on my own.

I got down in the muddy ditch. I looked for a place to set up a jack, hoping there was some way I could right my car, but there wasn't a place that was solid enough to set it up.

Just as I was giving up hope, I turned to see a man standing next to me. This surprised me as I had just looked up and down both sides of the road a moment earlier, hoping to see someone, but didn't.

He would have been hard to miss, too. He was six feet tall with a beard and looked to be in his thirties with olive skin. He was dressed like a bum but didn't seem to belong in the clothes he wore.

As crazy as it might sound, it almost looked like he was wearing a disguise.

He didn't waste time with pleasantries. Instead, he ordered me into the car. I did as he said. He then told me to put it in reverse. I tried to explain that I had already tried it; but he interrupted me and blurted out, "Back it up!"

At that point, he laid his hands on my hood. The car moved back onto the road smoothly without any trouble and without any scraping as if it were already on level road.

I was shocked. The car was downhill with the full weight of the engine hanging over the end of the road. This man didn't have the strength to lift it back on the road. Yet, there I was, ready to make the trip down the road. I got out of the car to talk to him and offered him a ride back into town. He refused. I then asked if I could pay him, but he asked only one thing of me.

"Just praise God," he said.

I got in the car to start it up but decided I couldn't just leave it at that. I got out again, but the man was gone. I had a clear view of anywhere he could have run within those few seconds, but he was nowhere to be seen.

In the end, all I could do was what he asked. I praised God, and drove down the road.

—Anonymous

My Angel is Always Near

When I was a very little girl, I had an experience that shaped the rest of my days since.

I was in my room, trying to sleep, but I kept tossing and turning. As I tried to force myself to sleep, I suddenly saw a strange golden glow beginning to form in a dark corner of the room. It got brighter and brighter until eventually I saw a small girl emerge from the light. She was golden, too, and floated toward me. As she got closer to me, I became terribly afraid.

Just as I was about to scream, she reached out and touched my chest with her hand. Almost immediately, I felt this warmth fill me. I felt comforted and totally at peace—completely safe and protected.

Although her mouth never moved, she spoke to me. She said that I was not ever to be afraid because she would always be beside me. She told me about some things that were going to happen in my life, but made it very clear that even though I wouldn't see her, I would never be alone throughout any of it.

When she was certain that I understood her, she began to pull away. I told her I wanted to go with her, but she looked at me lovingly and said that my time had not yet come. She smiled and disappeared.

I fell into the deepest, most peaceful sleep after that, knowing that she wasn't far away.

I kept this to myself for many years for fear that people might think I had lost my mind. Recently though, I was comforting a friend who had lost his little sister and decided to tell him the story, hoping it would bless him. As I spoke, I could see that his doubts were smoothing away. Knowing someone who had met an angel proved to him that our physical lives are just the beginning of our forever, and that what is next is beautiful for those that believe.

Since then, I've decided to tell everyone I can that no matter what happens in life, good or bad, your angel is always near.

—JOAN W.

Then the Angel of the Lord went further, and stood in a narrow place where there was no way to turn either to the right hand or to the left.

– NUMBERS 22:26 –

An Angel's Hands

My daughter, Kathleen, was only 15 years old and was a little too young to be dating anyone seriously. She had a boyfriend, though, and I did my best to go along with it as long as I knew where they were at all times. This worked out pretty well most of the time, but on my father's birthday I had a lot going on, which put me in a position to trust a little more than I normally would have.

My youngest daughter, Therese, was already with my dad, while my son, Paul, was at baseball practice. I still had a cake to get and party favors to find, so when Kathleen asked if she could go with her boyfriend to pick up his brother, I reluctantly agreed. As she was leaving, I added a provision that she had to wear her seatbelt and come directly home afterward.

I rushed out to get Paul first but took the highway instead of the roads that I would normally take. I don't know why I did this, as it was out of character for me. I guess it just seemed like a better idea to miss all of the stop signs.

I made it to the ballpark without a hitch; and, once Paul was in the car, I went to the bakery where the cake was waiting. I was pleased with myself as it felt like I was making good time and that everything was happening on schedule. As we were getting in the car though, the sound of distant sirens caught my attention. Whatever had happened must have been bad because those sirens were joined by other sirens and then still more. We saw paramedics moving toward the scene along with a fire truck and police.

As I drove away, I got a sick feeling and told Paul that someone needed our prayers. I wondered if there was a fire or a bad car accident.

At one point, I had to stop to let even more emergency vehicles pass, so I took that moment to pray as well.

I should clarify here that I firmly believed in angels. There was no doubt in my mind as to their existence. I was so sure of this that I had even named my guardian angel "Martha." So at that moment, while I was praying, I asked Martha to go to the aid of the people caught in the accident.

My next stop was my parents' house to drop off the cake. As I got to the door, my father met me. He seemed relieved.

"What way did you come from?" he asked. Before I could answer he went on, "On the way you usually go to pick up Paul, there was a horrible accident on that back road. I know you always go that way. I heard that someone was killed. I was afraid it might have been you!"

Kathleen, I thought.

My heart sank. I didn't say anything as I didn't want to worry my father, but I got in the car and drove home as quickly as I could. When I arrived at the house, the lights were out. This was a sure sign that nobody was home as Kathleen is the kind to turn on nearly every light in the house. "It was Kathleen," I said out loud.

I rushed in and checked our messages but nobody had called. I breathed a sigh of relief thinking that was a good sign. Kathleen always told me that I was paranoid, so I hung on that thought. *I'm just being paranoid*, I told myself. *Paranoid*. Just then, the phone rang. It was a friend's mom who worked in the emergency room of the hospital. She told me that three kids were in an accident, and they were being transported to the hospital. She then broke the news that Kathleen was involved. Beyond that, she couldn't give me any details.

I didn't take the time to call my husband or my parents. Paul and I just tore off to the hospital.

When I pulled into the driveway, a paramedic that I had known for years was walking toward me. He was crying.

"I'm sorry... so sorry," he said.

It was all a fog after that. I don't even remember going into the hospital. The next thing I knew I was talking to a doctor in the emergency room.

"Do you believe in God?" he asked.

My knees gave way.

"No," he said as he helped steady me. "You don't understand my question. Do you believe in divine intervention?"

"Yes," I said weakly.

He smiled at me. "Do you know what shirt your daughter was wearing tonight?"

I couldn't speak. I just shook my head from side to side.

He told me to go down the hall and look. "Your daughter is blessed with angels, and so are you. There is no way your daughter should be alive, let alone with only a few scratches."

I went in to see her and there she was lying peacefully on a bed waiting for more x-rays. When I reached her we both embraced and sobbed in each other's arms. When the tears became laughter, I remembered what the doctor had said about her shirt. I unzipped her jacket and pulled it open to read the words through many tears.

"Jesus saves."

After the hospital had checked for any kind of serious internal injury, all three kids were treated and released. On the way home, Kathleen began to tell me about what had happened.

"It was weird, Mom. When we were just a couple of blocks from getting in the accident, I remembered that we had not put on our seatbelts. I told everyone to belt-up or my mother would kill me. Just then a car came toward us in our lane. He swerved, and we got hit on my side of the car. We got hit a total of three times because our car kept slamming into other cars. While this was happening, I felt my boyfriend's little brother holding my shoulders, keeping me firmly in the seat."

She stopped for a minute, as if wondering if she should tell me the next part. "When I looked behind me though, nobody was there. It turned out that his brother was thrown from the car with the first collision."

She paused for a moment to let the truth of what happened settle in.

"It was an angel, Mom. I know it."

The next day we inspected the car and saw that it had been virtually split in half on my daughter's side. Witnesses said that the other car was moving at a great rate of speed, maybe in excess of 90 miles per hour. The police report said that the door had been found 50 feet away, and the metal holding the seatbelt to the chassis of the car was completely detached. The only thing holding my daughter to the seat and keeping her safe were those hands—the hands of an angel.

Today Kathleen is 23 years old with a child of her own. I'm sure that it's only a matter of time before she tells her baby the story of the guardian angel. I'm just as certain that she'll take after me and pray from time to time for a little help of her own when her daughter needs a hand.

—BARBARA PITCAVAGE

From End to Beginning

———❦———

I have only recently begun to tell family and friends about this incident for fear that they would think I had lost my mind. What happened to me was so wonderful and real that I couldn't keep it to myself, knowing that it could comfort others.

When I was only six years old, I was outside riding my bike when a bright light appeared in front of me, causing me to stop. I stared into it and began to make out a figure within it. Then facial features came into focus.

He smiled at me.

He told me not to be afraid. I probably should have been, but I wasn't. I truly felt completely safe.

"Do not be afraid," he said. "There is nothing to fear. Never fear anything."

As he spoke, no part of me was scared. I felt no fear. None. I was completely calm and at peace. Even more than that, I felt love.

It was the purest love I had ever known, and it was more than something I felt on the inside. It covered me and permeated me, running over me and through me at the same time.

When it was over, I decided not to tell anyone about it, but many times when I was young, whenever I would run into a frightening situation, I would think back on that moment and find myself comforted and cleansed the way I was back then.

As I grew older, I learned how to cope with things the way that adults do and didn't find myself in that many frightening situations. While I remembered the event, I didn't need that cleansing power anymore and forgot what it felt like.

Then my father died.

This is something that hurt me deeply. I missed him and felt alone. While I no longer depended on him to take care of me, there was still some fear that came with facing life without a father.

But then I remembered the angel's words to me, and the same feeling that I had experienced when I was only six years old returned. I felt total peace, total love, and total acceptance in exactly the same way I had felt it back then. I realized then that my father was feeling that same total peace, total love and total acceptance that I had found in the light so many years ago.

So now I pass along the story to you.

Pass it on.

—Cynthia Manke

FACE TO FACE WITH AN ANGEL

It seems as if most of the time, angels are content to be unseen, just beyond the veil of the physical realm. From time to time though, there is no other way to do their job but to make themselves known and show their faces.

It was a beautiful day. The skies were blue and clear, and the flowers were just beginning to bloom away the last signs of winter.

I was on my way home with my best friend, Tammy. We had spent our day off shopping and driving mountain roads. As registered nurses, our jobs can be somewhat stressful. So today was a welcome break from our normal routine. We were having a wonderful time together.

This changed in a handful of seconds as we went around a corner to see a truck on our side of the road—heading directly for us at 70 mph.

Initially I thought he was just doing an illegal pass and would pull back hard into his lane, but he was asleep at the wheel and just kept coming.

I looked to the left (in what should have been his lane) and there were cars coming. To the right there was a guard rail and a sheer drop down the mountainside.

"He's going to hit us!" Tammy yelled out.

Before I could say anything, the truck slammed into us. We hit the guard rail so hard that we bounced off of it, slid across the other lanes and hit the opposite guard rail as well.

When the car came to a stop, I was bleeding from everywhere. My femur had been pushed through my hip socket, causing severe pain.

As a nurse, I knew enough about medicine to know that I wouldn't last long.

My friend Tammy was also injured, although less severely. She kept me alive by tending to me, and talking to me to keep me awake. Looking past her own pain, she unselfishly and lovingly focused on me.

The pain was incredible. It was beyond the point of what I could take. I wondered how long it would be before help would find us and if I could last that long.

Just then, through the broken glass of the rear window, an angel appeared to us. I thought I might be hallucinating as the result of some head injury; but when I looked at Tammy, it was clear that she was seeing him too.

"It is okay," he said. "Jesus is praying for you, and you will be okay. It is not yet your time to go. You are safe now, and I will stay with you until they take you."

At that moment, the pain became bearable and I felt perfectly at peace. I was not afraid.

The angel did not speak again but stood guard.

Just down the road a CHP officer who had been writing a ticket came to the rescue, preceded by an off-duty officer who had called in for paramedics and firemen. The police didn't seem to see the angel when they got to the scene, and when the ambulance arrived, they worked around him as if he weren't even there.

My friend Tammy later told me that the angel did not leave when they took me away, but stayed with her too, until another ambulance arrived. It was at that moment she saw him disappear.

Later my friend and I both contacted the first responders to ask them if they had seen the angel, and nobody knew what we were talking about. He had appeared just to us to keep us alive for whatever it was that we were supposed to do with our lives.

Since then, I have always felt God's presence and the presence of that angel. They have seen me through other tragedies, too. The difference is that now I no longer have to see my angel to know he is there.

—ANONYMOUS

A Glimpse of Heaven

———◆———

I was sleeping soundly when I felt three gentle tugs at the foot of my blanket. I was alone in my apartment, so I should have been alarmed, but I was in a deep enough sleep that I thought that I'd imagined it.

Rolling over, I pulled the covers up to my neck and was out again.

Three more tugs.

Most men in this strange situation would probably be in a panic, but for some reason, I dismissed it as a dream and slipped back into sleep.

Three more tugs.

This time, I was aware that someone was in my room and trying to get my attention. Oddly enough, I didn't feel any fear as I sat up to see that a most beautiful man was suddenly in my room. He wasn't at the foot of my bed but standing by the wall. A white light surrounded him from head to foot. The intensity of the light obscured some details, but I was able to see that his face and hands were bronze colored and that his body was in perfect shape.

He wore a white robe with a white sash made of beautiful material. I couldn't place what kind of fabric it was because I'd never seen anything quite like it before.

He stood nearly 8 feet tall. I know this because my ceilings were 8 feet high, and he filled the room, standing straight with his hands down by his side.

"Do not be afraid," he said. "It is the voice of God. Read Isaiah, man of the patient realm."

Suddenly, in the blink of an eye, he was by my side. Next to me he looked even bigger as he reached out, scooped me up in his mighty arms, and held me like a baby. I felt completely safe and comfortable as he cradled me.

I heard a whizzing sound and felt like we were in motion. When the sound was over, I was no longer in his arms, but standing next to him on a very rich and beautiful earth. Only, it wasn't like the earth as I knew it. As my bare feet rested in the soil, I sensed that something about it was different.

We walked into some kind of outdoor marketplace. There were others just like him walking around, too. They were all very tall and beautiful, wearing the same white robes and sashes. Some of them were by themselves, on their way to or from some business. Others were walking in twos, like we were.

We stopped in front of a booth that reminded me of something you might see at a carnival. Inside of it there were three rows of large, handcrafted vessels. My angel was standing to my right and told me to choose something. I replied that I had no money.

"You don't need money here," he said. "Everything is free."

Just then, I heard that same whizzing sound from before, and we seemed to be in motion again, traveling at a great speed. The next thing I knew, we were standing by my bed, next to each other. He slowly leaned down, scooped me up in his arms and placed me back on the mattress. As I felt gravity pulling on my body again, he was gone.

I laid there perfectly still for the longest time until finally I got out of bed, flipped on a light, and began to write down what had just happened. Even though I knew I'd never forget the words of the angel, I wrote them down anyway.

Isaiah. Man of the patient realm.

Over the next few days, I read the book of Isaiah. Even though it was written 800 years before Christ, some folks call it the fifth Gospel because it so accurately details the life of Jesus.

In those beautiful words, I found hope, love, faith and confidence that God had heard my prayers and that He was indeed watching over me.

—ANONYMOUS

Praise him, all his angels;

praise him, all his hosts!

– PSALM 148:2 –

On a Mission From God

As a member of the Spiceland Volunteer Fire Department, I was normally on the rescue end of tragedy; so it was strange and surreal when, on an ordinary evening, I found that I was suddenly the one who needed help.

While driving down some unfamiliar roads at night, I was in a terrible accident. The left side of my jaw was shattered, and the other side was broken in two places. My left lung had been ruptured and collapsed. By the time the paramedics arrived, I was near death, unconscious and no longer breathing.

I was taken to the Methodist Hospital in Indianapolis, Indiana, where I was put on life support with a "trach" in my throat, a feeding tube in my stomach, and hoses down to my lungs. I was in a coma for a week and a half.

Members of the fire department came to the hospital. They'd seen people as bad as I was and confided to me later that they honestly did not expect me to live. My parents and my wife came as well, hardly ever leaving my side.

One day, when my wife was alone with me and holding my hand, a very young boy walked into the room. This surprised my wife as I was in was the Neuro-Critical Care Unit where visitors were carefully restricted and monitored. Moreover, children were not even allowed without special arrangements being made.

The boy came in, looked at me, and then left without saying a word– as if he had something to do. Despite the fact that nurses and doctors were walking up and down the hall, no one seemed to notice him.

A short time later, he returned. "Hi," he said to my wife.

"Hello," she replied.

"He was in a wreck?"

"Yes."

He was calm and spoke in a comforting tone. "He is going to be okay. I am an angel. I'm on a mission from God. This is what I do. Can I pray for him?"

When my wife told him that he could, the boy walked over to the other side of my bed, took my hand, and began to pray. My wife watched him as he spoke to God, and his face began to give off a soft light. When he finished, he looked at my wife and smiled the most beautiful smile.

"He is going to be okay," he repeated. "I'm an angel from God. This is what I do."

He left, and she never saw him again.

After a few days, to the surprise of everyone, I came out of the coma, and not long after that, I was walking.

I didn't see my angel while in my comatose state, but when I look down at the hand the angel held, I smile, knowing that I was the objective of an angel on a mission from God.

—TOM HILL

FINDING OUR WAY

When I was a young boy, my parents raised my two sisters and me to believe in God, taking us to a local church of about 100 members. In that little church, I learned about values and the importance of faithfulness, honestly, integrity and trust. It was a very special place.

So when my father passed away peacefully in his sleep at the age of eighty-six, my family decided to hold the memorial service at that church instead of the funeral home. My father had been loved by so many people there that it just seemed right.

I had gone to the church early to finish setting things up when I happened upon an elderly woman. I had never met her before, so it seemed odd that she would be in our little church. My father was loved and well respected by so many people in the community that I figured she must have been one of the many people he had helped along the way.

I asked if she was a visitor or a friend of one of our members. She replied, "Yes, I'm a visitor." She smiled at me and turned to walk into the sanctuary. I watched her as she made her way down the aisle. She moved so slowly that I thought about helping her, but before I could ask, she took a seat at one of the pews.

I turned away to go back to what I was doing when I felt the air stir past me. I turned and looked around to see what caused that curious sensation, but no one was there. I was also shocked to see that the woman had vanished.

I literally rubbed my eyes like people do in the movies when they think their eyes are playing tricks on them. The "visitor" was gone.

I was stunned. Even a person who could move normally wouldn't have been able to get past me unnoticed. She had moved so slowly before that there was just no rational explanation as to where she could have gone.

I struggled with this strange event for the rest of the day. I described her to others and asked if anyone knew her, but no one knew the woman about whom I spoke. I looked for her at the service, and later on at the grave site, but I never saw her again. I was baffled and disturbed by what had happened.

A few days later, my sisters and I got together to discuss Dad's will. We hadn't even talked about it in the days prior to this, as we all needed some time to deal with the loss, but then came the unhappy task of taking care of his estate.

We knew Dad had a will somewhere, as he joked about it often and wasn't the kind to leave things up in the air. He was a self-made man and conservative in his spending, so we knew that he had a little money socked away somewhere.

My sister, Deanna, took the initiative and began the search for Dad's will. She looked in all of the normal places like file cabinets, important folders, drawers and the like. She found nothing, so now we all joined in the effort. It was starting to worry us. We didn't want the state to get involved, and it just wasn't like Dad to misplace something as important as a legal document. Yet it was nowhere to be found.

Eventually, confused and discouraged, we decided to call it a night as we had to be at church early the following morning for Sunday worship. I laid in bed for a while thinking about Dad and his will when the image of that slow moving little old lady came to mind. I fell asleep thinking of her.

The next day when I arrived at church, I went to sit in the area where the "visitor" sat on the day of Dad's memorial service. As I sat there thinking, I saw something sticking out of one of the hymnals. It was a "Smoky Mountains Visitor's Guide." I picked it up and began thumbing through it when I noticed a receipt for flowers. Written on the back of the receipt was one word.

Maps.

After the service, I began to wonder about that little lady and if the guide had belonged to her. This only added more mystery to the situation.

Later that night, while I was thinking about all that had happened, the image of my dad's map book came to mind. I began to wonder if maybe. . .

I went to his office, pulled the map book from the bookcase, and next to the map of Tennessee, where the Smoky Mountains are, was Dad's will.

I firmly believe that the "visitor" was an angel, leading us to the map when we needed to find our way.

—Gary Bell

THIS IS ONLY A TEXT

~◦~

Nobody who ever texted while driving thought the end-result would be an accident. Yet over half of all traffic fatalities are the result of distracted drivers. The one second spent switching a radio station, text messaging, or taking a sip of coffee can be the exact second that a disaster could have been averted—and wasn't.

On the day of my personal incident, it was another beautiful morning in Southern California, which can be a distraction in itself. I made a stop to pick up a cup of coffee on the way to work, but it burnt my lip when I tried to sip it. It would cool down enough for me to enjoy on the last half of my drive though, so I found a way to manage steadying it without a cup holder and made my way to the 405 freeway.

As I merged into traffic, I was glad to see that the lanes were clear. Sometimes that freeway could be a parking lot, especially during rush hour or when an accident had happened. Even the smallest fender bender could cause rubberneckers to slow down for a glimpse of someone else's misfortune. Today we were good though, and running at full speed without a care in the world.

As I was enjoying the drive and thinking about giving that cup of coffee a second chance, I heard my cell phone announce a text message. I reached into my purse and dug around, feeling for the phone's familiar shape. As I found it, I quickly navigated the menu with glances up at the road, until I found the message. Before I could read it, I heard a man's voice whisper in my right ear.

"Watch out."

At that moment, I looked up to see the brake lights on the car in front of me. I was too close to the car to hit my brakes, but some kind of force took over the steering wheel, and my car swerved into the right lane. I was fortunate there wasn't a car in that lane because I could have been killed.

Hot coffee spilled everywhere.

Ahead of me, I saw that there had been a terrible accident where a car spun out and was left facing the wrong way on the freeway. To think that I was only a misplaced fraction of a second away from being added to that accident! The thought still gives me chills.

By the time I got off of the road, I was shaking and thanking God and my guardian angel for those words of warning. Had I been looking down, I would have most certainly plowed full speed into the cars already stopped ahead of me. To this very day I pray to God and remember my guardian angel when I get into my car.

The good thing to come out of the 'almost accident' is that I definitely won't text while driving anymore. I hope my message will serve as someone else's word of warning.

—Monique G.

In the Twinkle of an Eye

———❦———

I wanted a baby. It was my life-long dream to be a mother and something I knew in my heart that I could do well. Yet after years of trying to conceive, I was not able to get pregnant. Even fertility drugs failed to make it happen.

When it became clear that something was wrong, my doctor recommended that I have an outpatient radiological procedure to examine my reproductive system. I was very nervous about it, but held on to the hope that they would figure out what was keeping me from getting pregnant and fix it so that I could have a baby.

Sadly, this was not the case. After a series of tests, my doctor delivered the crushing news to me. He said conceiving a child naturally just would not be possible and suggested that my husband and I consider adoption or possibly in *vitro* fertilization. It was the worst possible news. I was devastated.

It was all that I could do to keep it together as I was escorted into the dressing room where I had left my clothes. I shut the door, sat down on a chair near a small restroom and began crying uncontrollably. I replayed the doctor's last words to me. How could I tell my husband? What would I do now that my hope was gone?

Afraid that someone would come in and find me this way, I found refuge in the tiny restroom. I let the tears fall freely as I began to get dressed. My anguish reminded me of ocean waves—just as one subsided another would begin to rise, covering me in sorrow.

I finished getting dressed and tried to steady myself for the trip out to the car. Just as I opened the door to the tiny restroom, I was surprised to see a woman standing there with a sympathetic look and extended arms.

"You do not know me," she said, "but I think you need a hug." I never got the chance to pull away from this kind stranger as she took me in her arms. She caressed my head as I let the pain I felt come bubbling to the surface again. I felt no shame. Something about her comforted me.

Even though she was a stranger, I told her what had happened to me. She responded by taking my face into her hands and asking me if I believed in God.

"Yes, but why ME? It's so unfair!" I replied. "I was put on this earth to be a mother!"

I continued to cry as she explained that many people have a purpose in life and to think of all of the children already on this earth that have no home. She told me that God has a plan for all of the parentless—children and childless couples alike. She looked straight into my eyes and said, "God has a plan for you, too." With that, she gave me one last embrace and went into this bathroom that I had just occupied.

I went to the chair nearest the door exit to put on my shoes, enjoying the sense of peace that this woman had given me. I felt a little bit stronger and I was thinking clearly again.

I decided to wait for her to come out of the restroom so that I could thank her. But as I sat there, I remembered a very important errand that I needed to tend to. Not able to stay any longer, I decided to knock on the bathroom door to thank the woman, hoping my behavior did not seem rude. There was no answer. I knocked louder but still no response.

I started to worry about her. After all, she was at a doctor's office, too, and for all I knew she was facing some medical issues herself. I tested the door knob to find it was unlocked. Ever so gently I opened the door to find that the room was empty. She was nowhere to be found!

I knew immediately that I had been touched by an angel. The meaning of the moment wasn't lost on me. She was especially appointed to visit me on that bleak October day to remind me of God's unfailing love. Ever since, I have always felt special for witnessing this miracle myself.

After that day, my life changed. I began to work on being faithful. I began to take steps to improve the quality of my life by looking for all of God's blessings, no matter how small. I focused on Him and being grateful to be His child. We decided to adopt and focused on being thankful for whatever way that God was going to bring us a child.

Just then, while in the process of being interviewed by an adoption agency, I discovered I was pregnant. A few months later, I gave birth to a beautiful little boy.

Not a day goes by that I do not thank God for Nolan. Not a day goes by that I do not think of the angel who reminded me that God had a plan for me all along.

—SHAWN SHEPPARD

The angel of the Lord came

back a second time and

touched him...

– I KINGS 19:7 –

Angel on the Stairs

Many years ago, when I was just six years old, my father took me to the doctor for a serious middle ear infection. The doctor's office was located in a very large Victorian style home that dated back to before the Civil War.

We had just left the doctor's examination room and were standing in the hallway when my father picked me up and sat me on his shoulders. I could see rays of the evening sunlight through a pane of glass located above a closed wooden door.

I looked through the window and saw a woman with pure white hair. She was dressed in white and smiled at me as she came through the door and went down the stairs. The only thing was, she didn't seem to be walking. She floated just above the steps, moving smoothly past us. As she went by, I felt this perfect peace wash over me and through me. It was an amazing feeling.

Later that evening, I asked my father how a lady could float down the stairs like that. He laughed and told me it was not possible. But I knew what I saw. Even now, some thirty years later, I remember it vividly.

Last year, my father died of cancer. As if coming full circle, the doctor's office we had gone to three decades before was now a funeral home. In fact, the very room where I was examined for my ear infection was the same room where the casket rested with my father inside.

When I got there to say my final goodbyes to him, I remembered that woman who floated down the stairs like an angel. The memory of that moment filled me with that perfect peace again and helped me through another difficult moment in my life.

—Emma Taylor

Protection from My Own Mistake

⊷

The thing about drinking alcohol is that it shuts down the part of your brain that knows better. We say things we don't mean, or say things we mean but shouldn't say. We make mistakes in a single night that we must live with for life. What makes people think that they can drive a car when they can't walk a straight line? The smart thing to do when you know you are going to be turning off your good judgment with a few drinks is to leave your car at home. So many of us don't take that precaution, and live or die with the consequences.

While I was a young woman still in my twenties, I went out drinking and dancing with some friends on a Saturday night. I had way too much to drink and shouldn't have been driving, but I got behind the wheel of my little Chevy anyway and took off for home.

At one point, I was going well over the speed limit, doing 80 to 90 miles an hour, when I felt the car slow down by itself. At first I thought I was running out of gas, but my gauge showed that I still had fuel. Puzzled, I pumped the gas pedal and got it back up to speed, only to have the car mysteriously slow down again. This last time though, the engine continued to decelerate until it finally died, leaving me to coast off to the side of the road.

When I came to a stop, I tried to get the car started again, but the engine didn't even turn over.

So there I was, a young, drunk girl, forced to sit helplessly in the car by the side of the road. Anybody could have seen me, and I would have been powerless to defend myself. Thankfully, a police car came first and asked if I needed a ride.

I let him take me home and explained what happened with my car. He told me that it was a lucky break for me because there had been a tanker-truck oil spill about a mile from where I had broken down. Two cars had slid off the road into the ditch before flares and barricades could be set up to redirect the traffic.

I knew right then that if I had hit the oil slick going as fast as I was driving, I would have killed myself.

The next day, my dad and a mechanic friend of his went out to see if they could fix my car. It started perfectly and never slowed down like that again.

To this day I thank God for sending angels to watch over me. I never drove again after drinking alcohol. I didn't deserve angelic protection, but since God gave me another chance, I'm using it to warn others not to drink and drive!

—ANONYMOUS

HE IS LISTENING, ALWAYS

───❦───

The long hand of the clock was making its agonizingly slow trek toward 5:00. What is it about the end of the workday that makes time slow down, especially on Fridays?

Although I had no plans, just having a weekend off was enough for me. When the time came to leave, I was like a horse coming out of the starting gate. I didn't even bother pushing my chair under my desk as I darted toward the exit. In my mind, my weekend started the moment I went through that door.

I felt myself relax as soon as I stepped outside. To make the whole thing even more dramatic, the Lord was in the middle of creating one of the most breathtaking sunsets I had ever seen. The sky was like a watercolor painting in motion, with vibrant hues of orange, red, yellow, purple and blue. It was so beautiful, I decided to sit down on the curb and watch God paint the horizon.

Overjoyed, I could feel the powerful presence of God all around me, so I decided to ask Him if He could show me an angel. I know from scripture that they are all around us, but that normally we don't see them. While He had already given me enough to be in awe of, I sent up a prayer anyway. I was open for anything—a glimpse of an angel in the sky—even a cloud in the shape of an angel would have been fine.

Just then, a man spoke to me. "Young lady?" he asked.

I looked beside me to see that he was an older man with a kind face and a warm smile.

"Yes sir," I replied.

"Are you a child of God?" he asked.

For a few seconds, I was stunned. It was an odd question to ask a perfect stranger, especially one who was lost in thought. As a believer though, I took that as a sign that my prayer was being answered.

I replied, "Why, yes, aren't we all?"

He smiled again and, without saying a word, he sat down beside me, and we watched the sunset together.

When the spectacle ended, he asked, "It was beautiful, wasn't it?"

I nodded as he stood up and departed, leaving me full of joy and grateful for God's answer to my prayer. It also made me feel especially good that even when God is busy painting, He is listening.

—ANGELIA FROST

Do not forget to entertain
strangers, for by so doing
some have unwittingly
entertained angels.

– HEBREWS 13:2 –

Near Drowning

My mother and I went to Coney Island in the summer of 1963. I was excited to be going as I loved the ocean and was a pretty good swimmer for an eight-year-old.

However, on this particular day, the waves were coming in a little harder and higher than usual; so my mother thought it would be best to skip the water for the day and just take in some sunshine instead.

The allure of the ocean was too much for me though, so I waited until my mother had found a friend to talk with. Then I headed out for the waves to enjoy a quick dip.

As I splashed into water, I found that the waves were quite large, but nothing I couldn't handle. I spotted my mom in the distance, motioning for me to come in. She had a concerned look on her face.

Suddenly, a huge wave covered me. I began to scream as I felt the power of the angry ocean pull me under. Water poured into my lungs, and I began to panic, knowing that I could die in the next few seconds.

Then, as loudly as if I were on the surface, I heard a voice that sounded like it came from woman. "Calm down," she said. "Hold your breath and swim toward the light."

I opened my eyes in the salty water and looked up. I had been pulled down so deep that it seemed like it would take forever to get to the surface, but I held my breath and swam toward the light as I was told. The whole time, the woman's voice continued to instruct me and encourage me until I made it to the top.

The waves kept coming as I gasped for air, but the voice continued to coach me, letting me know how to get out of the water. At one point, she told me just to lay back and float. When I did, the water carried me to the shore.

When I got there, my mother took me in her arms and held me as I coughed and threw up water. The only lifeguard on duty was running up towards me and told my mother he had seen me go under. He told me I was a very lucky girl because there was a moment when I had been under for so long that I shouldn't have been able to survive.

I did, though, thanks to presence of an angel who knew how to guide me into the light.

—MARY PLAN

LISTEN WELL

Many years ago when I was still struggling to get by, I had an encounter with an angel that has shaped all of my days since.

I was poor and driving a beat up old Mustang that had no business being on the road. When you don't have money though, you don't have a lot of choices either, so I had to find a way to make it work. Sometimes I had to give up eating to pay for repairs; but, I needed a car to get to work, so that was just the way it was.

One day, I was going to a friend's house when I stopped at a red light. There was an auto repair business on the corner; and, as I looked at it, something weird happened—I saw a vision.

With the clarity of a movie on a theater screen, I saw my Mustang explode. As the images played out, I heard a voice that was as clear as day, telling me to get the car into that garage.

"But I can't afford it!" I said out loud.

The "vision" cleared as I shook my head. I was beginning to think I was going crazy. Ignoring the advice of the voice and the vision, I waited for the light to change and went on to my friend's house.

After a few hours, when it was time for me to go, I got into my car, put the key in the ignition and turned it. I felt a jolt that shook the whole car as the engine blew up.

I sat there, unable to move for a moment, watching in shock as fire engulfed the front end of my car— just as my vision had foretold. People came outside to see what happened. Someone got a fire extinguisher as I got out of the car unharmed.

I don't know a lot about cars, so I can't say what actually happened under the hood; but afterward, when I spoke to a mechanic about it, he said that the whole car should have exploded. It was a miracle that I was able to walk away from the incident.

I know that angels protected me that day. They tried to warn me; and when I didn't obey, they shielded me anyway.

Next time I hear that voice, I'm listening.

—JADZIA SHABO

A LUCKY BRAKE

I loved driving fast. Despite lots of close calls where I should have lost my life, I usually found myself pushing the limits on my motorcycle anyway. Aside from the obvious problems with this driving style, there was yet another added danger. Specifically, there was no way to anticipate the mistakes of other drivers on the road.

One day, I got a wake-up call that changed my driving for good.

I was going very fast, enjoying the power of my motorcycle on the open road. With no traffic in sight I was able to really push it. Then, for no reason at all, I got on the brakes hard.

I was braking as hard as I possibly could, almost locking up the tires. The only thing that kept me from laying the bike down was the years of experience I had driving it.

I skidded to a stop just as a car blasted by me at a high rate of speed. It emerged suddenly from a concealed side street and was so close that it nearly grazed me as it went by. When it was gone, I sat there in shock.

I'd heard stories of people being warned of impending doom with voices in their head, but I didn't hear or see anything that day. I had no reason for getting on the brakes that hard. None! Yet, if I hadn't brought myself to a stop, I would have certainly been killed.

I believe it was my guardian angel who knew that I didn't have time to do this the old-fashioned way, so he saved me by flipping the subconscious brake switch and letting my instincts take over.

These days I'm driving a lot safer so that my guardian angel doesn't have to work so hard to keep me around.

—GAVAN BROOKS

THE LITTLE MIRACLES

When I was 19, I had some problems with my pregnancy and wound up giving birth to my daughter four months early. As with all premature births, her survival depended on medical intervention to keep her alive. She was fed intravenously, and given antibiotics to combat infections. She had oxygen tents to keep her breathing, and monitors watched over her vital signs as she laid there in that lonely, sterile, clear, plastic bassinet.

The weeks went by and turned into months as the hospital staff worked hard to get my daughter's strength and weight up. Finally, after eight long months, she was cleared to go home.

Even after all that time, she was so tiny compared to other babies and still required monitors to watch over her even once she was home.

She would cry a lot, too, so I would rock her. I remember one day when all my efforts just weren't working. I had walked her and rocked her to no avail. Nothing seemed to comfort her. Finally I put her down to make a bottle, hoping that a full stomach might lead to a partial night's sleep for all of us.

When I returned, she was not crying. She was sleeping peacefully. Mothers often jump right on these moments for a quick nap, as they are often few and far between; but before I could give in to some much needed rest, I looked next to her and saw something I didn't expect to see. There was an angel pin on her pillow. I didn't know where it had come from—I had never seen it before. Upon closer examination I saw an inscription that said, "I'll always love you and be with you forever. Amen."

Whether an angel placed it there, or it had been there all along, I never knew. To me it's always been easier to believe that an angel placed that pin there than to believe that a protective mother would miss some-thing like that on her baby's pillow. Believe what you will. All I know is this: if angels are messengers, that message on the pin was just what I needed to see.

My daughter is now six years old, and she keeps the pin close by as a reminder that none of us are too small to get God's attention.

—DEONA MONTGOMERY

Walking Out of the Furnace

~~~~

During this particular time, I was working as a midwife in the Houston area, helping women to give birth in their homes.

One evening, while visiting a client, I was paged by another mother who had gone into labor six weeks early.

In my line of work, sometimes you had to move quickly. So I jumped in the car and took off down the freeway toward the woman's home.

Although the speed limit was a brisk 55, there were still traffic lights every so often. As I approached one such intersection, the light changed to yellow, so I slowed down.

Unfortunately the person behind me didn't see the light change or recognize that I was slowing down. My guess is that he was looking over his shoulder to make a lane change. Regardless, he rear-ended me at 70 mph, causing a huge explosion. The impact combined with the explosion to throw me into the path of an oncoming Camaro that slammed hard into me.

The inside of the car was orange with the flames. The back seat was completely engulfed in fire. I tried the door but it wouldn't open. Apparently the collision with the Camaro had wedged the door shut, leaving me trapped in a growing inferno. I pulled the handle and shouldered it as hard as I could to get it open, but it wouldn't budge.

A fireman who happened to be following us down the road had witnessed the whole event. He called for help right away but didn't have the tools to help me.

Meanwhile, I was still stuck in the car. It dawned on me that I would probably be burned alive, so I prayed to God for escape. Suddenly the door fell open, and I fell onto the pavement. I ran away from the car and, at about 30 yards, turned to see the front seat entirely consumed in flames.

What was odd was that I didn't even smell like smoke. I wasn't burned anywhere. Despite being trapped for so long in a burning car, I was fine.

I believe that an angel pulled that door off the hinges, in answer to a prayer.

—ANONYMOUS

Raphael

It all started innocently enough. My son was on his way to school, crossing the street where he always did, when another child came up from behind him, snatched his backpack and took off running. My son chased after him and was so focused on this other boy that he didn't see the car approaching. Before the vehicle could stop, my boy was struck and sent flying 30 feet into air to land in the middle of the street.

Someone I knew was at the scene, so I was called almost as soon as it happened. My husband and I were on the road already and just a short distance away, so we rushed to our child, getting there before the ambulance arrived.

I felt sick as I saw my son, crumpled in the street, surrounded by onlookers. I ran to his side and wanted to pick him up and hold him, but I couldn't risk hurting him more by moving him. All I could do was pray, wait, and hold his hand.

When the ambulance arrived, the paramedics quickly worked to get him on the gurney and secured him to the point where he was immobilized and safe from further injury.

They let my husband ride with them, leaving me to follow in the car. Once we arrived at the hospital, my husband remained with our boy as I sat alone in the waiting room. While I probably would have been crying anyway, it was good not having an audience as I dealt with the pain. This day had started out so normal; and, in the flash of a brake light, I was at the hospital, begging for a miracle.

As I struggled with all of the emotions a mother can feel at such a time, I began to notice that the light in the room was getting brighter. I looked around to see if a lamp or overhead light was just malfunctioning, but the light seemed to emanate from the empty space in the room. With every second it was getting brighter until finally it turned into the brightest white light I had ever seen.

Instead of being alarmed, just looking at the light calmed me somehow. I found assurance in that illumination that my son would be okay. As it grew brighter, I saw a vision of an angel named Raphael, slowing down the car. How I saw this "vision" I don't know. How I knew the angel's name, I don't know either. I just knew. After that, I had no tears to cry because my fear was replaced by faith.

My son wound up being fine. It wasn't long before he was able to come back home with us, having suffered no long-term effects from the accident.

As time went on, I ended up doubting what I had seen in that waiting room. Time has a way of explaining away the miraculous events we experience. That goes all the way back to the Bible. The Israelites had seen the plagues that led to their freedom from Egypt; and yet, somewhere along the way to the Promised Land, they had forgotten what they had witnessed.

I did exactly the same thing and eventually dismissed what I had experienced as some kind of panic-fueled delusion—the wishful thinking of a traumatized mother worried about her son.

Sometime later, however, when I talked about the whole thing with my boy, he told me the most curious thing. He said that he didn't remember much about the accident, but he did know that someone was with him the whole time.

He said his name was Raphael.

Right then I decided to write down my story in hopes that it would encourage anyone who ever wondered if there is anything on the other side of our faith.

Angels do exist and so does the One who created them.

As a side note, the name Raphael means, "the God who heals." No surprise there.

—JUNE P.

So he went out and followed
him, and did not know that
what was done by the angel
was real, but thought he was
seeing a vision.

– ACTS 12:9 –

Do you have an angel story that you would like to share?
If so, contact the author through her website at:
Lynnvalentinebooks.blogspot.com

If you enjoyed this book, Hallmark would love to hear from you.

PLEASE SEND YOUR COMMENTS TO:
Hallmark Book Feedback
P.O. Box 419034
Mail Drop 215
Kansas City, MO 64141

OR E-MAIL US AT:
booknotes@hallmark.com